My name is...
Albert Einstein

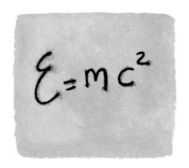

$$E = mc^2$$

BARRON'S

Original title of the book in Spanish: *Me llamo...Albert Einstein*
© 2004 Parramón Ediciones, S.A.,—World Rights
Published by Parramón Ediciones, S.A., Barcelona, Spain

Name of the author of the text: Lluís Cugota
Name of the illustrator: Gustavo Roldán

Translated from the Spanish by Eric A. Bye, M.A.

Project and Production: Parramón Publishing
Editorial Director: Lluís Borràs
Editorial Assistant: Cristina Vilella
Text: Lluís Cugota
Illustrations: Gustavo Roldán
Graphic Design and Layout: Zink Communications, Inc.
Production Director: Rafael Marfil
Production: Manel Sánchez

All inquiries should be addressed to:
Barron's Educational Series, Inc.
250 Wireless Boulevard
Hauppauge, New York 11788
www.barronseduc.com

ISBN-13: 978-0-7641-3391-6
ISBN-10: 0-7641-3391-8

Library of Congress Catalog Card No.: 2005929509

Printed in Spain
9 8 7 6 5 4 3 2 1

Hello...

Celebrity always overwhelmed me. I considered myself to be a calm person who loved his work and world peace, and I never got used to the avalanche of reporters, the flashes from their cameras, and the tons of questions about my private life, which of course I never answered. One day, I became so overwhelmed by the press that I just stuck my tongue out to show my disgust. And wouldn't you know it, that photograph became one of the most famous ones in history.

Many times I was asked how I came up with my theories, where I got the ideas, and how I managed to simplify the most complicated things. The answer is simple. I have always said that you have to try things ninety-nine times in order to succeed on the hundredth attempt. I never considered myself better than anybody else, and it's clear that I'm not the smartest man in the world, as some have said. But I have always worked with determination, motivated by curiosity and the desire to know. I have a certain tendency to ask myself questions, and when a thing starts going around in my head, I need to see it clearly and understand how it works. I have no material ambitions, and I seek neither honor nor fame. But I am convinced that every one of us can contribute a little bit to the knowledge and the welfare of humankind. I tried to do that for seventy-six years, one month, and four days... And sometimes I feel like I succeeded.

A Brilliant Childhood

I was born one sunny morning in March of 1879, on the fourteenth, in Ulm, a city located on the banks of the Danube, in the south of Germany, in the state of Württemberg. It seems that I was a pudgy and slightly stubborn baby, as my grandmother often reminded me. My father was named Hermann, and he had an electrical supply shop on the cathedral square. My mother, whose name was Pauline, loved music and played the piano very well.

We lived in Ulm only a very short time. It was a peaceful town, with lots of churches, some of them very ancient and of great artistic value, such as the cathedral, a tremendous Gothic temple with the highest bell tower in the world, rising a full 500 feet (161 meters). Many years later, in 1922, they put my name on a street in the city, Einstein Street. That was very exciting. But let's not get ahead of ourselves...

When I was one year old, we moved to Munich. There we joined Uncle Jacob, my father's brother. Uncle Jacob was an engineer, and he had designed a new type of electrical generator. He was sure that electricity was the future, and he convinced my father to join him in the task of illuminating the capital of Bavaria. Uncle Jacob thought that could turn into a good business, since at that time Munich had more than 300,000 residents.

I started to speak at the age of three, "a little late for a genius," as some of my biographers would later remark. Of course, I was speaking before that age, but the problem was that nobody understood me. Back then I would say things twice, so that

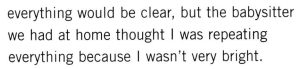

everything would be clear, but the babysitter we had at home thought I was repeating everything because I wasn't very bright.

When I was six, we went to live in a large house with a huge yard, near the family's electrical appliance store and power plant. The factory already had nearly two hundred workers.

I also started going to school with my sister Maia, who was two years younger than me. There I learned to read and write. I didn't find it too difficult, even though at first they said that I changed the order of the syllables as I read some words.

But in the Saint Peter Catholic school, we were the only two Jewish children. I remember that on one occasion a bunch of somewhat bigger children chased me and threw stones at me simply because I was a Jew.

I couldn't understand why they did it. Maybe because I didn't like sports very much and because I hated the military parades that were so widespread all through Germany at that time. What I really liked was construction toys and compasses. My father reminded me of that many times later on...

A Mysterious Animal Named X

I must have been around four or five years old when one day my father showed me a compass. I was fascinated by the movement of the needle that always pointed north, faithfully following the direction of the earth's magnetic field. Of course at that time I could see only that its movement was caused by some invisible, mysterious force. Something fascinating stirred my curiosity, and as a result, it had to be studied, and the secret had to be revealed. Even at that young age, I was learning the importance of asking questions—curiosity has its own reason for existing.

Uncle Jacob's favorite story about me, which he told time and again, involved the day he taught me the Pythagorean theorem; he said I wouldn't rest until I had demonstrated it by myself. There must have been something to that, since I had never even opened a math book in my life! Uncle Jacob was a good man; he helped me do my homework, and he told me wonderful stories. For example, he told me that algebra was a lighthearted science in which the object was to capture a mysterious animal that we called *x*.

I remember that I loved geometry. I felt a special attraction to it, and to music. Although my mother played the piano very well, I preferred the violin. Let's just say it was easier to handle—much easier, in fact—and I was always fascinated by its sound. I became interested in Mozart and his sonatas, but I also played pieces by Bach and Schubert. I was probably about five or six years old. I don't think I was ever separated from my violin. It went with me everywhere. It was, in fact, an inseparable companion throughout my entire life. And I say it was a companion because for some reason I always called it Lina.

In 1889, at the age of ten, I entered the Luitpol Institute.

It was amazing to think that thirty years earlier, the great philosopher Friedrich Nietzsche had studied at that very place. I was tremendously interested in philosophy, mathematics, and physics, and perhaps less in arts and literature, although I did fairly well. I must admit that I got good grades. But sometimes I thought the teachers had it in for me. Discipline was important there, and I had a fairly independent nature, so I often had problems—let's just say that I was a little undisciplined! Once, a teacher told me in a very serious tone of voice, "Einstein, you are an intelligent boy, but you have one major defect: you never take advice from anybody."

At the Institute, everyone had to study religion. I studied Christianity carefully, and at home I studied Judaism; both the Bible and the Torah, one of the holy books of the Hebrews, were my spiritual sources.

My Early Fascination with Science

According to the custom observed among Jewish families, one day a week we would invite some needy person to dinner. For months, Max Talmey, a Russian Jew who was as poor as he was hungry, came regularly to our house. Max was studying medicine, and he would bring me all kinds of science books. I loved them, but they posed a serious conflict for me. Religion and science frequently contradicted one another. I spoke with Max about all this for long periods of time. We talked about all the subjects from mathematics to physics and philosophy. I think it was then that I began to think in scientific terms and pushed aside the religious beliefs. Science provided me with some convincing answers, whereas religion provided only questions and ideas that were impossible to prove. I think that's when I started refusing to be told what to do and mistrusting all authority.

In 1893, when I was fourteen years old, things started to go badly for the Einstein electrical company, since the city government awarded the job of providing power to Munich to a different company. My father and Uncle Jacob had to lay off their workers; they sold the company, and the following year, the whole family moved to Italy. Well, the whole family except for me, because I had to stay in Munich to finish school.

Those were very sad months.

As a student boarder at the Institute and alone in the city, I watched with uneasiness as German society increasingly leaned toward National Socialism, the early stages of the Nazi Party, and more and more against the Jews.

In addition, the Institute was torture. The teaching methods were old-fashioned; so many times I intentionally asked the teachers difficult questions. They didn't know what to say to me. I saw that this bothered them. Once I exasperated the Greek teacher so much that he kicked me out of class.

I had spent Christmas vacation alone in December 1894. Then, a week later, I suddenly boarded a train headed for Milan, which was near where my parents were living, in Pavia. Before leaving, I renounced my German citizenship. I didn't want to be a citizen of a militarized and authoritarian state. I wanted to become a Swiss citizen, but because I was a minor, I spent a few years as a person without a country. This episode bothered my father very much, but for me, well, at first it seemed a little strange, but then it didn't matter very much.

Riding a Beam of Light

The time I spent in Italy was one of the happiest periods in my life. Pavia, near Milan, was a beautiful place with a large square and many medieval palaces. It was next to the Ticino, a gentle and navigable river. There my father and Uncle Jacob had built a new electric power plant. I continued studying mathematics on my own, and I pondered and posed questions to myself on topics that interested me, such as what would happen if it were possible to ride a ray of light or travel at the speed of light. I still had so many questions. Although I was just a young man, I knew that the most beautiful thing that we can experience is the mysterious.

I spent a wonderful year, but in the end, the good life also came to a close. My father insisted that I begin to study electrical engineering, but I didn't pass the entrance exam for the Zurich Polytechnic School, one of the most prestigious institutes in Europe. That failure really bothered me. In spite of it all, since I had done a great job on the mathematics part of the exam, the director of the institute suggested that I get some better preparation in a good school and come back the following year, when I would be eighteen and have the necessary knowledge. He recommended the school in Arau, Switzerland. So that's where I went.

I really liked the year I spent in Arau. The capital of the Swiss province of Argovia was a small city, but it had a wonderful view of the Alps. The school used modern educational methods. In addition, I roomed in the house of one of the teachers, Jost Winteler, a person of very fine character, the father of seven children, and a great lover of birds. We began a relationship that lasted a lifetime.

Ah! And I experienced my first love, for Marie, one of the professor's daughters. Marie and I would play piano four hands, and we had a great time. Some afternoons I played the violin until my fingers hurt. I also greatly enjoyed studying, so when I applied to the Polytechnic School once again, I easily passed the entrance exam.

A Taste for Simple Things

Starting advanced studies in a new school was very exciting for me. In my first class, I met Mileva Maric, the only girl in a class of eleven students. Mileva was a few years older than me, and her parents were Serbian refugees. We became friends, and very soon we started going out together. We also studied calculus, geometry, and mechanics together. Mileva was a very intelligent girl with a strong and independent character, just like me.

Those years of training in the Zurich Polytechnic School were really instructive. I studied James Maxwell's theories of electromagnetism. I cut the classes that I considered boring and relied on Marcel Grossmann, who was a true artist at taking—and loaning—class notes. I continued to despise everything related to discipline, and preferred to study on my own the things that interested me. Besides schoolwork, I also liked sailing, which I did every chance I got, as well as attending concerts and musical parties.

I stayed away from student parties and other social events that I considered a waste of time.

At one point I had to decide whether to concentrate on mathematics or physics, and I opted for physics. It was said that I had a special talent, for I was capable of following a trail that would lead right to the basic principles, pushing aside the other things that creep into your mind, distract you, and keep you away from what really counts.

At the age of twenty, I applied for Swiss citizenship. It was granted two years later in 1901. In fact, it was that same year that I published my first article in the magazine *Annals of Physics*. It dealt with capillary action, that is, the reactions of liquids in contact with solids. It wasn't much—just a naive approach to a fairly unimportant topic.

In Bern, and with Mileva

When I finished my studies, I immediately sought work. I applied to be a teacher in many schools and universities, but all I got was a couple of temporary jobs. Things couldn't go on like that. Once again, my good friend Marcel came to the rescue. It turns out that his father knew the director of the Swiss Office of Intellectual Property, an organization that people commonly referred to as the Bern Office of Patent Registration. I got a temporary contract as a third-class official. It wasn't much, but at least it was a dependable job. In February of 1902 I settled in Bern, and in June I started to work in the patent office with a salary of 3,500 francs a year (about $2,700)... not much even in those days.

In October of 1902, my father died. I think that was the first time I ever cried. He had given me the greatest gift—the gift of curiosity.

Two friends and I established the Olympia Academy, the purpose of which was to discuss philosophy and important questions. We met once a week and had a good time discussing a little of everything. I devoted the free moments I had in the patent office to studying and thinking. But I had to hide my books and my notes when anyone came around—a rather awkward situation.

In 1903 Mileva and I got married. We lived in the old part of the city, near the clock tower. Bern is a very pleasant city. The following year our son Hans Albert was born. All this time I was writing, and in 1904 I sent several works to the magazine *Annals of Physics*, three of which dealt with thermodynamics.

1905: Four Is a Magic Number

I have to acknowledge that 1905 was my year of grace. I studied and wrote quite a lot, and I had the good fortune to have four articles published in the magazine directed by Max Planck, a very well-known physicist. In March, I sent an article on light to *Annals of Physics*—specifically, on the photoelectric effect and *light quantums*, which later became known as photons. The photoelectric effect involves the emission of electrons by a metal when a beam of light is directed onto it. This effect confirmed my theory that even though light behaves like a wave, it is made up of tiny bodies of energy, or *quantums*. That was a bold assertion for that time. But when it was later confirmed, many of my colleagues considered me the founder of quantum theory. That's not why I wrote it; but thanks to that article, years later I was awarded the Nobel Prize in Physics.

The second article, which I sent to the same magazine in May, focused on Brownian movement, which is nothing more than the

chaotic and constant
motion of small particles on
the surface of liquids. It got its
name from a Scottish naturalist from the middle of the
nineteenth century, Robert Brown, whose attention had been
attracted to the uncontrolled movement of pollen grains on pond
water. Think of how important it is for scientists to know about
the work of others.

So I demonstrated mathematically that this movement is caused
by the instability of the molecules of the liquid in question. This
was also a direct proof of the existence of atoms.

I entitled the third article, which the magazine received at the end of June, "On the Electrodynamics of Bodies in Motion." It described the theory of special relativity, a theory concerning time, distance, mass, and energy. The idea was simple, but it took me a long time to put it together. I wanted to demonstrate that space and time are relative to an observer. As the years went by, my example of the train became famous for explaining this idea. Let's suppose that we are traveling on a train that's moving at a speed of 50 miles per hour (mph). Nearby, outside the train, a friend watches what is happening. We roll a billiard ball along the corridor of the train in the direction of travel. For us, who are inside the train, the billiard ball is rolling, say, at

2 mph. However, for our friend who is watching this action from the outside, the billiard ball is moving at 52 mph, that is, the sum of the speeds of the train and the ball. In addition, according to the theory of relativity, the faster we move, the more slowly time moves. This means that as we approach the speed of light, space contracts. Does this all seem difficult to understand? Surely, if you are just beginning to learn about physics, it is. Do keep in mind that all science is nothing more than an enhancement of everyday thinking!

Before the end of that year, I sent another article to the magazine to complete the one on relativity. It was a brief conclusion of about three pages, but I was very satisfied with that work. I had

succeeded in establishing the equivalence between mass and energy by means of an equation as simple as $E = mc^2$. I think this is a magnificent formula. In fact, this very formula would make me famous! It allows us to understand how it is possible to obtain a tremendous quantity of energy (E) from a tiny mass (m), since the latter is multiplied by the speed of light squared (c^2), which will always give us a very large product, since the speed of light is no less than 186,281 miles (300,000 km) per second. Thus, tiny quantities of mass can be transformed into tremendous quantities of energy. This is the principle with which nuclear power plants would later work in order to produce energy. It also makes up the scientific basis of the atomic bomb, a terribly sad subject that I will talk about later. Now do you understand the

theory of relativity? Of course not, but if you try to see some of the parts, you may one day understand the whole!

Of all these ideas, the theory of relativity was the one that most interested my colleagues. The famous physicist Max Planck wrote me months later to tell me of his enthusiasm. The idea seemed wonderful to him. For several days I could hardly believe it. And you, my dear young readers…while you may find this difficult to understand now, you will understand much more when the study of science gives you the tools to unlock the mysterious!

Astronauts in the Streets of Bern

The following year, in 1906, I was promoted at work to second-class expert, and my salary was increased by a thousand francs ($770) a year. Some friends were surprised that a person with my interests would continue working in a patent office reviewing and filing other people's discoveries. I remember those years with fondness, since they allowed me to continue developing new ideas and writing them down in spare moments. In fact, while I was at the patent office I wrote twenty-five articles, and some of them—as we have already seen—were extremely significant for my scientific career.

Most of the ideas came to me spontaneously, through intuition, almost by chance… Like that day when, to clear my head a little, I looked out the window and watched the bustle in the street. Suddenly, somebody on an upper floor dropped something out the window, and I saw an object fall in front of me. I then thought that a person in free fall would not feel his or her weight— that is, the person would weigh nothing. See how imagination can often be more important than knowledge? But here's where knowledge can be applied to that imagination.

Obviously, I didn't try that in practice, but with time, others would have that very experience. For example, astronauts inside their spaceship, far away from earth's gravity, float in the air and weigh nothing. Gravity is the acceleration to which all bodies within a given gravitational field are subjected. So gravity and acceleration are equivalent...

But space and time also change in relation to gravity. The greater the attraction of a body, the slower time passes. And the greater the mass of the body that exerts the attraction, the greater the attraction and the slower the passage of time. Time is one more dimension of space. As a result, mass can bend space-time.

Light, Good Friends, and the City of Prague

In 1908 I was hired as an assistant professor at Bern University. It was not a very important post, and my salary came from the tuition paid by the students in my classes. Therefore, I didn't earn very much, I had to spend lots of hours teaching, and in addition, I didn't get along well with the rest of the professors. I spent a couple of months surviving as well as I could.

In September of the following year, 1909, I was invited to deliver an address at a science convention in Salzburg, Austria. I talked about "The Development of Our Concept of Nature and the Constitution of Radiation," which dealt with the corpuscular (minute particles) and undulating nature of light. I don't know if it was the subject or my presentation, but I don't think they understood me very well. So see, you are not alone! Luckily, I

met the best scientists of the country, and I corresponded with some of them for years.

That October, after having spent seven years in the patent office, I landed a job as an adjunct professor of theoretical physics at the University of Zurich, Switzerland. My life as a professor was beginning. Then Edward, our second son, was born. However, my relationship with Mileva, my wife, was beginning to become strained, and after so many years of happiness, it seemed that things weren't working as well as before.

In 1911, I was offered a full professorship at the German University in Prague, the capital of the Czech Republic. I was delighted to accept the position. The German University had separated from the Czech University after a long string of conflicts. Since I had no sympathy for National Socialism, the other professors didn't pay much attention to me. And as a German, I wasn't particularly beloved by the Czechs. In addition, the significant Jewish community in Prague was seeking my attention and my support. With all this confusion, I often locked myself in my laboratory and worked for hours and hours.

I was thinking about acceleration, the relativity of time, and the bending of light, for if light has mass, it must be attracted to a greater force... these issues kept me very busy. But I still wasn't interested in conventional society, and I often declined invitations to parties or just to have coffee; I preferred to go my own way and dress as I pleased.

Quantum Physics and Right Angles That Bend

That same year, I was invited to the First Solvay Convention in Brussels, Belgium, a high-level science meeting that was being promoted by the Belgian impresario Ernest Solvay. For the first four days of November, some twenty physicists from around the world discussed progress in physics. I think they were the largest group of Nobel Prize laureates assembled up to that time. We provided some momentum to the *quantum* theory and to relativity.

For me a *quantum* was a packet of energy, an essential component of matter. Quantum physics was useful to me in proposing a likely description of the infinitely small. That is, matter is composed of particles that may be there, which doesn't mean that they really exist, but rather that everything depends on a calculation of the probabilities. Interesting, isn't it? Well, you may think so soon! In addition, among the attendees, Madame Curie and Henri Poincaré, who were very influential at that time, expressed their support for my ideas. Thus I quickly became a man in great demand, and I was invited to go the universities of Utrecht, Leiden, Vienna, and Zurich as a professor.

In fact, I returned that same year to the Polytechnic School in Zurich, although it was now called the Swiss Polytechnic University. I couldn't refuse, since they had created the professorship of theoretical physics for me. I felt very much at home. In addition, I needed a little calm, since I was trying to demonstrate that gravity was an issue of geometry rather than of force. The geometry was a little special, where parallel straight lines may cease to be so in infinity, and the angles of a square are not straight, but rather curved. This is the so-called non-Euclidian geometry, which was developed by the German mathematician Bernhard Riemann. He, too, thought that the universe was a unified space-time system that could be described with this geometry, in which everything ended up bending. But the calculations were awful; so, as in the old days, I solicited the help of Marcel Grossmann, who was by now a mathematics professor at the Polytechnic University, and he was nice enough to give me a hand with the equations. See how we need other sources and experts to further our own ideas?

General Relativity and Space-Time

In 1913, Max Planck, permanent secretary of the Prussian Academy of Sciences, convinced me to accept a department chairmanship at the University of Berlin. He gave me total freedom to teach or do research. The salary was good, and of course I accepted. In addition, my cousin Elsa was in Berlin; for some time we had been writing one another and discussing so many things. In recent months, my relationship with Mileva had gotten worse. She was always sad and couldn't get used to our new life. She wanted nothing to do with a move to Berlin.

That same year, with Marcel, I published the article "An Outline of a Theory of Generalized Relativity and a Theory of

Gravitation," which was to become the first step toward the theory of general relativity.

Finally, we moved to Berlin in 1914. But in July, my good friend Michele Besso came to get Mileva and the children, and they returned to Zurich. I spent a few days in great sorrow. I was alone once again. That year another great sadness darkened the scene. World War I had broken out, and people were fighting and dying all across Europe. It was a disaster that caused me tremendous suffering. Thanks to my Swiss nationality, I was not required to collaborate with any German military regime. So I resumed my studies on gravity, and a few months later, at the start of November of 1915, I presented to the Prussian Academy of Sciences my work entitled "On the General Theory of Relativity." In nine pages I attempted to explain how time is a dimension in which all other phenomena occur, as if at every moment the universe were superimposing a copy of itself upon its same but earlier self, and all of the copies formed space-time, creating a complicated geometric figure

in which straight lines bend under the force of gravity.

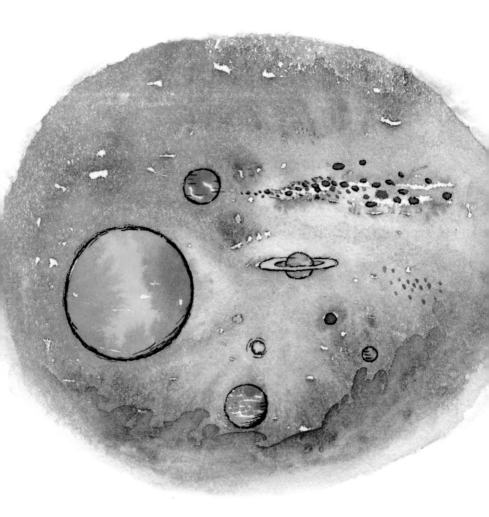

Thus, gravity was no longer a force of attraction between two bodies, but rather a property of space-time. Space-time was regulated by ten equations, all of which are quite complicated. All of these ideas together made it possible to create a solid basis on which to study the universe, and that would later turn into the new science of cosmology.

The Eclipse, a Burst of Fame, and Elsa

In 1919, fortune smiled on me once again. A solar eclipse brought me worldwide fame and great personal satisfaction. Finally, some of my theories would be tested in practice, and not only with some scribbling on paper. It turned out that Arthur Eddington, the famous British astronomer, was fascinated by my theories on the curvature of space-time. He was resolved to test them during the solar eclipse that year. To do that, he organized two scientific expeditions for the purpose of taking a good collection of photographs.

The theory of general relativity predicted a displacement of the stars closest to the sun during the dark phase of the eclipse. Eddington's measurements confirmed these predictions. I had never been so happy about an eclipse. And that happiness seemed to invade even the English press, which published the story with big headlines. The rest of the world followed the path blazed by the British journalists. All the newspapers became interested in my life and my work. In the course of a year, I appeared in many media—even though none of them really explained my theories logically, and they remained confusing to most people. In spite of that, I received many invitations to present seminars and speak at conferences.

I felt overwhelmed with all the attention. Relativity had become as popular as the Charleston (a famous dance of the time).

That same year, after living apart for five years, Mileva and I got divorced. She kept custody of the children, but I took care of supporting them. A few months later, on June 2, I married Elsa, who also had two children from a previous marriage. In this sense, it was a very happy year for me. But at the end of the year, my mother, who was very ill, moved in with us. Maia, my sister, also came to live with us. Mother died shortly thereafter, in March of 1920. Elsa was very tolerant, and she loved me so much. Our marriage was good for several years. Once she bought me a brush so I could comb my hair "properly," she said, but it didn't bother me to wear my hair long and messy.

Jewish Physics and American Hospitality

The social and political situation in Europe after World War I was very turbulent. I knew that the National Socialists had it in for me because I was a Jew. They said it was impossible for a Jew to make a discovery as important as the theory of relativity. These opinions made me laugh—and sometimes cry—since a human's brain has nothing to do with religion or the origins of a person's parents. In fact, the ardent supporters of National Socialism blamed the Jews for all their problems, including responsibility for the German defeat in World War I. In 1920 the anti-Semitic campaigns intensified. My theory of relativity was considered "a degenerate and incomprehensible science." I came to be the major representative of what they called "Jewish physics." They wanted to ridicule me, but nobody succeeded in disproving the equations, which most people didn't understand. I couldn't turn my back on my people. I defended them any way I could, wherever I went, and whenever necessary. So it wasn't too hard for Chaim Weizmann, the creator of the World Zionist Organization, who would be the first president of Israel between 1949 and 1952, to convince me to travel to the United States to collect funds for the construction of the first Hebrew University in Jerusalem.

The trip to the United States was wonderful. The journalists pursued us relentlessly from the moment we landed. I had to appear in many different places. I always spoke in German. I supposed that somebody understood me, in addition to the many German scientists who had to leave their country for political reasons.

I stayed in New York for several days. Princeton University awarded me an honorary doctoral degree. The trip was a success, and we managed to collect a lot of money for constructing the Jerusalem Medical School. In the United States, the Jewish movement was very strong.

Three Nobels in One

On the way home, in the spring of 1921, I made a stopover in England, where I gave several lectures. But the situation in Europe was getting worse day by day. In France, I had problems because I was German, and I had to go into hiding to escape the anti-German furor that had taken over the country. In Germany, the situation wasn't much better. I received death threats nearly every day. Given the situation, in October of 1922, I decided to bring the family together and spend a few weeks in Japan, where we had been invited. During the trip, when we were traveling on the coast of China, we received the news that I had been granted the Nobel Prize in Physics for the discovery of the law of the photoelectric effect.

This prize gave me considerable hope. It was tremendously satisfying for me. I found it strange that the 1921 Nobel Prize was awarded to me in 1922 and I couldn't get it until 1923. Thus, it almost seemed like three prizes instead of just one. I was told that the Swedish Academy granted the Nobel Physics Prize only for works that had been proven experimentally, so they didn't mention my theory of relativity.

In 1923, I visited Spain. On February 23, I arrived in Barcelona with my wife, and we stayed in the Quatre Nacions Hotel, a comfortable but simple establishment, but afterward we learned that they had originally reserved a room for us in the luxurious Ritz Hotel. When a public representative mentioned that to us, I answered that I was a modest citizen and that I had taken a room that was appropriate to my station in life. He seemed amazed by my words, but he was very kind to us. I gave three lectures amid great expectation, all of them dealing with relativity.

Troubles in Berlin and the Unification Theory

Back home, the economic situation in Germany was very bad. The National Socialists, or Nazis, kept gaining more power in the government. But there was a certain calm in Berlin... a deceiving calm, because at the end of 1923, a crowd led by Adolf Hitler took it upon themselves to loot the Jewish businesses in the city. Elsa, my wife, was scared to death. So we left for Leiden, Holland for a few days. We returned to Berlin six weeks later when the disturbances seemed to have quieted down a little.

In those years, physics got turned upside down with new theories and great new ideas. I had disagreements with people over quantum physics, and also tried to refute the principle of uncertainty and the principle of complementarity. Ah...much too detailed to go into here! Do find out more at your leisure! Then I left that "new physics" alone for a while and focused on putting together a theory that would unite the basic forces of the universe. But this task was not an easy one, either. Can you see how my mind was spinning with so much to think about?

I was so exhausted at this time that I had a major physical collapse from working so hard. It took me a whole year to fully recover my strength.

I Turn Fifty and the Nazis Burn My Books

I turned fifty on March 14, 1929. I was in Gatow at the house of my doctor and friend, sailing and enjoying the fresh air for a few days. They told me that my house in Berlin was nearly buried in flowers, congratulations, and telegrams sent from all corners of the world. My friends gave me a gift of a wonderful sailboat. The city of Berlin wanted to present me with a house by my favorite lake, but all the homes were occupied. After a few years, they finally gave me land and I had my own house built.

The following year, during the winter of 1930, I returned to the United States at the invitation of the California Institute of Technology. In Hollywood, I saw many movies that were banned in Germany, and I met Charlie Chaplin, a famous comedian. How he made me laugh! I gave several lectures and presented classes and seminars.

In July of 1932, the National Socialist Party won the elections. The atmosphere in Germany was becoming oppressive. On December 1, I attended the meetings of the Prussian Academy of Sciences for the last time. Four days later I took Elsa by the hand and, accompanied by my assistant and my secretary, we applied for visas in the United States consulate. In a few days we were in Antwerp, Belgium, and very soon we headed for the United States.

In January of 1933, the Nazis assumed power. The following month they burned Parliament and blamed it on the Communists. I was in California, and I thought it appropriate to announce publicly that I would not return to Germany. When the winter was over, we returned to Europe and stayed in a small town in Belgium, where I was protected by an express order from the king, for he was afraid that the Nazis would try to kill me.

In Germany they took away my bank accounts and my property. They burned my works and tried to disprove my theories. All Jews were fired from their academic positions, and many were persecuted. More than a thousand department heads and professors were forced out of the country.

The ones who left saved their lives, but the ones who stayed sacrificed theirs. In the face of so many atrocities, I again renounced German citizenship. I didn't want any association with that cruelty. I was so critical of Nazism that the German Jews themselves accused me of provoking the issues and advised me to soften my statements, since Hitler was using my words to stir up racial and religious hatred even more.

A Night in the White House

In October of 1933 we arrived in Princeton, a quiet town in the state of New Jersey. The university in this town was very famous, and the best students attended it. It also had an Institute of Advanced Studies that had been constructed three years earlier; it was to be my workplace until the end of my days. We moved into a large two-story house with a yard. Life returned to a certain amount of peacefulness.

In 1934, the president of the United States, Franklin D. Roosevelt, invited me to spend a night in the White House. It was a perfect evening. I had a wonderful time, and the president spoke fluent German, so we were able to converse pleasantly on many subjects of interest.

My research continued. I resumed the critique of quantum mechanics, which I had put aside after my first discussions with Niels Bohr. Things were going fairly well for us.

In 1935 we bought an old colonial mansion that was so close to the university that I could walk to work. We began to fill it with the books and furniture that we had been able to bring from Germany.

In 1936 my friend Marcel Grossmann died, and in December of the same year, Elsa also lost her life. My soul was ripped apart in pain and sorrow. After that, all I could think of was to dedicate myself fully to my work. Perhaps if I kept my mind occupied I would stop feeling so much sadness...

In 1938 the German writer Thomas Mann came to Princeton as a guest professor.

We saw each other frequently during the two years he was there. Together we wrote several articles against Nazism and we presented lectures favoring peace and condemning intolerance. Still, Hitler stood his ground. He had already taken over Czechoslovakia and was preparing to invade Poland. Things were looking worse at every turn.

My Most Famous Formula and the Most Deadly Bomb

Following the works of the Italian scientist Enrico Fermi, and the experiments of the German scientists Otto Hahn and Fritz Strassmann, Bohr speculated on the possibility of causing a controlled reaction to release a great quantity of energy. The race to create the atomic bomb had begun. Then some old friends explained what would happen if the Nazis got the atomic bomb before the Americans. They were so disturbed by this possibility that on August 2, 1939, we sent a letter to President Franklin Roosevelt in which we suggested the use of nuclear energy and the construction of large atomic bombs before the Nazis accomplished this.

I signed that letter because I was outraged over what was happening in Germany and in Europe. I had always been a firm pacifist, but now I was supporting the use of force. I don't know if the president read that letter, but history would unfairly consider me the "father" of the atomic bomb. I very quickly moved to the sidelines of that atomic research, which was named the Manhattan Project, and I was always critical of the use of atomic energy for military purposes.

The Persecution of the Unifying Dream

At the age of sixty, one of my main endeavors was coming up with equations to relate gravity to electromagnetism. I was convinced that all the forces of the universe were controlled by the same laws. However, I couldn't figure out how to do it. I could understand gravity by means of geometry, and electromagnetism through waves and particles; but how was I to combine the two concepts? I searched for the right formulas for years; sometimes I thought I had found them, but I always ended up recognizing my errors. I tried to keep in mind my belief that anyone who has never made a mistake has never tried anything new!

In the meantime, in 1941 in Trenton, New Jersey, I was granted United States citizenship, even though I still kept my Swiss citizenship. It was a brief but very emotional ceremony. That year I performed a concert—violin, of course—to benefit children.

In December, the Japanese bombed Pearl Harbor, the American naval base in Hawaii. The United States declared war on Japan, and World War II became much more complicated than it already was.

The Road to Eternity

In 1948, Mileva died in Zurich, Switzerland. My sister Maia was very ill, and many afternoons I would read to her aloud to keep her company. My health wasn't very good, either. I was feeling the effects of old age. They operated on me and told me some news that I already knew: my heart, liver, and digestive system were in bad shape. Still, in 1949 we celebrated my seventieth birthday in style. They even organized a conference to commemorate all my discoveries.

In 1951, Maia died of pneumonia. The following year Chaim Weizmann, who had brought me to the United States for the first time and had been the first president of Israel, also died. The Israeli government offered me the presidency of the country. This offer was very emotional for me, but I had to decline the honor, since I didn't think I was strong enough for such a high position, and I didn't consider myself qualified for it.

I knew that I had only a few more years to live. When I looked at myself in the mirror, I saw a tired old man with a sad face, wrinkled skin, long hair, and a bushy mustache, but still willing to struggle for his ideals. Along with the philosopher Bertrand Russell, I signed a declaration in favor of world peace and

against the danger of nuclear war. I kept in contact with the authorities of Israel to prepare a declaration of peace with the Palestinians.

But my time had come. On April 15 they took me to Princeton Hospital. I knew that I was going to die, and three days later, on April 18, 1955, I did. Finally I could rest in peace. I left all my letters and manuscripts to the University of Jerusalem. I left my violin to my nephew Bernhard. I left instructions to cremate me and scatter my ashes in a secret place, perhaps on a lake or the ocean. But nobody could know where. I didn't want my grave to become a tourist or pilgrimage site. My desires were carried out.

However, they took out my brain and my eyes. They wanted to study them to see if they were like everyone else's. They found that they were. Of course—what else could they expect?

Years	Einstein's Life
1879–1890	1879 He is born on March 14 in Ulm, Germany. 1880 His family moves to Munich. 1881 His sister Maia is born. 1889 He enters the Luitpol Institute in Munich.
1891–1900	1894 He leaves the Institute and travels to Italy. He renounces German citizenship. 1895 He fails the entrance exam for the Zurich Polytechnic School. He enrolls in the Swiss School at Arau. 1896 He enrolls in the Zurich Polytechnic School. He meets Mileva Maric. 1900 He graduates from the Polytechnic School.
1901–1910	1901 He is granted Swiss citizenship. 1902 His father dies in Milan. He starts work in the Federal Office of Intellectual Property Patents in Bern, Switzerland. 1903 He marries Mileva Maric. 1904 His first son, Hans Albert, is born. 1905 He discovers the photoelectric effect. First publication on the theory of relativity. 1909 He leaves the patent office and accepts a department chairmanship at the University of Zurich. 1910 His second son, Edward, is born.
1911–1920	1913 He publishes "Outline of a Theory of General Relativity and a Theory of Gravitation" with Marcel Grossmann. He is elected a member of the Prussian Academy of Sciences in Berlin. 1916 He finishes the general theory of relativity. He begins new research into gravity. 1919 During an eclipse, his theory on the bending of light in a gravitational field is confirmed. He divorces Mileva and marries his cousin Elsa. 1920 He is named department chair at the University of Leiden, Holland.
1921–1930	1921 He is awarded the Nobel Prize in Physics for the discovery of the law of the photoelectric effect. He travels to the United States. 1923 He travels throughout England, Spain, Czechoslovakia, Palestine, and Japan. 1927 He attends the Solvay Conference. 1929 He turns fifty.
1931–1940	1933 The Nazis confiscate his property and put a price on his head. He is named professor in the Institute for Advanced Studies at Princeton. He settles permanently in the United States. 1936 Elsa, his second wife, and his friend Marcel Grossmann die. 1939 He sends a warlike letter to President Roosevelt. 1941 He is granted U.S. citizenship.
1941–1950	1946 He assumes the presidency of the Vigilance Committee of Atomic Scientists. 1948 Mileva, his first wife, dies. He publishes "A General Theory of Gravitation." 1950 He makes his will.
1951–1960	1952 He declines the presidency of Israel. 1954 He falls ill; he suffers from liver failure, anemia, and weakness. 1955 He dies in Princeton on April 18. He is cremated.

History	Science/Technology	Arts/Culture
Creation of the Triple Alliance involving Germany, Austria-Hungary, and Italy. Formation of the Second International in Paris.	Thomas Edison invents the incandescent electric lightbulb. First electric locomotive. High point of telegraphy and electromagnetism.	Pablo Picasso and Charlie Chaplin are born; Albert Einstein will meet them in 1930. Dostoyevsky dies.
War in Melilla and war in Cuba. Assassination of Cánovas del Castillo. Creation of the International Tribunal of the Hague.	Henri Becquerel discovers radioactivity and Wilhelm Röntgen discovers X-rays. Sigmund Freud publishes *The Interpretation of Dreams*.	Rudyard Kipling publishes *The Jungle Book*. Friedrich Nietzsche and Oscar Wilde die.
The first Nobel Prizes are awarded. Alfonso XIII is crowned king of Spain. The Sixth Zionist Congress calls for a Hebrew state in Palestine.	The first Mercedes automobiles appear in Germany. First flights of the Wright Brothers. Robert Koch, discoverer of the tuberculosis bacillus, dies.	Giuseppe Verdi dies. First exposition of Picasso in Paris. The architectural and decorating style Modernism flourishes. Jules Verne and Leon Tolstoy die.
World War I (1914–1918). Creation of League of Nations. The Russian Revolution breaks out. Worker unrest in Spain.	First uses of neon light. The Ford Model T becomes the first mass-produced automobile. Roald Amundsen conquers the South Pole. Alexander Fleming discovers penicillin, the first antibiotic.	Manuel de Falla premieres *Love the Magician* in the Madrid's Lara Theater. Miguel Delibes is born. Rubén Dario, Edgar Degas, and Gustav Mahler die.
Mussolini enters Rome with the Black Shirts. First National Socialist convention in Munich. Hitler publishes *Mein Kampf*. Lenin is president of the USSR.	Charles Lindbergh crosses the Atlantic nonstop. The insulin hormone is isolated. First daily television broadcasts in England.	Premiere of *The Jazz Singer*, the first sound movie. Herge publishes *Tintin in the Land of the Soviets*. International expositions in Barcelona and Seville, Spain.
Adolf Hitler, Reich's chancellor. Franklin D. Roosevelt, president of the United States. Spanish Civil War (1936–1939). World War II (1939–1945)	Flight around the world. The Golden Gate, the suspension bridge in San Francisco, is opened. Sigmund Freud and Santiago Ramón y Cajal die.	Jacinto Benavente is awarded the Nobel Prize for Literature. Enrico Caruso, Franz Kafka, and Antoni Gaudi die.
Japan bombs Pearl Harbor. Atomic bombs on Hiroshima and Nagasaki. Cold War and Korean War.	Enrico Fermi constructs the atomic battery. The first aerosols appear. First nuclear fission bomb.	Jean-Paul Sartre publishes *Being and Nothingness*. UNESCO and UNICEF are founded. Walt Disney premieres *Bambi*.
Dwight Eisenhower, president of the United States. The Warsaw Pact is signed. Elizabeth II, new queen of England.	First tranquilizers. Massive vaccinations against polio. James Watson and Francis Crick decode the structure of DNA.	Premiere of Welcome, *Mr. Marshall* by Luis Garcia Berlanga. Jorge Negrete and Eva Peron die.

My name is...

is a collection of biographies of people with universal appeal, written for young readers. In each book, a figure from history, science, art, culture, literature, or philosophy writes in an appealing way about his or her life and work, and about the world in which he or she lived. Abundant illustrations, inspired by the historical time period, help us become immersed in the time and the environment.

Albert Einstein

A native of Ulm, a city in the south of Germany with a magnificent cathedral, Einstein was named the "man of the century" by *Time* magazine. But why? Even though he didn't appear especially brilliant as a child, he soon showed his interest and his ability in reflecting on the great problems of modern physics. Then his work on light, electrodynamics, energy, space, and time made him world famous, since they confirmed theories from the past or solved fascinating puzzles of physics. Despite his far-reaching contributions to knowledge, he was a man of flesh and bone, and he liked to play the violin.